JAZZGUITAR
ARPEGGIOSOLOING

A Practical Guide To Soloing With Essential Arpeggios For Jazz Guitarists

TIMPETTINGALE

FUNDAMENTALCHANGES

Jazz Guitar Arpeggio Soloing

A Practical Guide To Soloing With Essential Arpeggios For Jazz Guitarists

ISBN: 978-1-78933-374-9

Published by **www.fundamental-changes.com**

Copyright © 2022 Tim Pettingale

Edited by Joseph Alexander

www.fundamental-changes.com

Over 12,000 fans on Facebook: **FundamentalChangesInGuitar**

Instagram: **FundamentalChanges**

For over 350 Free Guitar Lessons with Videos Check Out

www.fundamental-changes.com

Cover Image Copyright: Shutterstock, johnnyraff

Contents

Introduction.. 4

Get the Audio... 6

Chapter One – Major 7 Arpeggios.. 7

Chapter Two – Minor 9 Arpeggios... 23

Chapter Three – Dominant 7b9 Arpeggios.. 38

Chapter Four – Minor 7b5 Arpeggios... 51

Chapter Five –7#5b9 Arpeggios.. 63

Chapter Six – Major ii V I Arpeggio Vocabulary... 77

Chapter Seven – Minor ii V i Arpeggio Vocabulary.. 85

Appendix – Fretboard Maps.. 93

Introduction

Arpeggios are a mainstay of jazz guitar soloing vocabulary. While scale runs have their place and can be impressive, overuse them, or fail to be creative with them, and they can sound boring and robotic. Arpeggios, on the other hand, beautifully spell out the chord changes and ground our melodic lines in the harmony. Most jazz standards have rich harmonic progressions, so the ability to seamlessly articulate those changes with arpeggio-based lines is a great skill to have.

Arpeggios are the building blocks of great melodic ideas in jazz, and in this book we're going to thoroughly learn the *most important* arpeggios for the jazz guitarist. This book isn't a grimoire of arpeggios that shows you dozens of shapes but leaves you to work out how to apply them musically. Neither is it an exhaustive reference guide to every possible arpeggio from plain to the exotic. Instead, after years of listening to and studying the legends of jazz guitar, presented here are the most frequently used, must-know sounds in jazz guitar.

So, rather than study the minor 7 arpeggio, we'll look at the minor 9, because the 9th interval is heard so frequently in the playing of the greats; rather than study the straight dominant 7, we'll look at the 7b9 – a sound that became iconic in the creation of bebop; and so on...

Throughout the book, as well as completing a thorough workout on each arpeggio, we'll build towards soloing over the two most important sequences in jazz: the major and minor ii V I. Having instantly useable language to play over these two sequences will solve 90% of your jazz guitar problems!

Here are the individual arpeggios we'll cover:

- Cmaj7
- Dm9
- G7b9
- Bm7b5
- E7#5b9

The first three make up the major ii V I.

The next two begin the minor ii V I sequence (and the Dm9 ideas you learn can be transposed to Am9).

The last two chapters feature dozens of lines of varying difficulty you can play over these two sequences. Notice too, that these sequences are in relative keys (C Major and A Minor), so you're also covered when it comes to playing tunes that contain them both (such as *Autumn Leaves*).

The method

As we work with the arpeggios, each chapter will follow the same format:

- First, we'll learn the basic box shape patterns for each arpeggio
- Next, we'll learn extended patterns that use more of the range of the neck
- Then we'll move on to *arpeggio connections*. These are lines that connect together arpeggio shapes across the fretboard and help you learn more about each arpeggio's fretboard geography

- Next we'll play a selection of arpeggio lines that avoid starting from the root note. These are important for "disguising" the arpeggio and they sound more like melodic lines than patterns

- Finally, we'll introduce *passing notes* and see how it's possible to spice up our arpeggio lines with chromatics

By the end of the book, you'll have grown your jazz vocabulary considerably, and have a bank of solid ideas to draw on in every soloing situation. Throughout, I'll explain the approach behind each line, so that you can develop the tools to create your own melodic ideas from scratch.

I hope you have fun with it.

Tim

Get the Audio

The audio files for this book are available to download for free from **www.fundamental-changes.com.** The link is in the top right-hand corner. Click on the "Guitar" link then simply select this book title from the drop-down menu and follow the instructions to get the audio.

We recommend that you download the files directly to your computer, not to your tablet, and extract them there before adding them to your media library. You can then put them onto your tablet, iPod or burn them to CD. On the download page there are instructions and we also provide technical support via the contact form.

For over 350 free guitar lessons with videos check out:

www.fundamental-changes.com

Over 12,000 fans on Facebook: **FundamentalChangesInGuitar**

Tag us for a share on Instagram: **FundamentalChanges**

Chapter One – Major 7 Arpeggios

Major 7 chords

In jazz, major 7ths are by far the most prevalent type of major chords used, so it's essential to become fluent at soloing with the major 7 arpeggio. The exercises in this chapter will help you to learn it thoroughly, but also get the most out of it creatively.

It's worth remembering that, when soloing, you can play major 7 arpeggio ideas over every chord in the ii V I sequence (i.e. C major arpeggio ideas over Dm7 – G7 – Cmaj7).

Of course, it's more interesting to spell out each chord in the ii V I, but consider this your emergency backup strategy. When you've just been introduced to a new jazz standard and have seconds to analyse it before playing it on the bandstand, it's always best to reduce the harmony down to the main tonal centres. The major 7 arpeggio is your friend here, so it's worth knowing inside out.

In this chapter we'll learn a set of arpeggio shapes that are useful to the jazz guitarist. We're going to drill them with these goals in mind:

- To learn the arpeggio in several different locations on the neck

- To learn it in a way that will enable us to make better fretboard connections and use more of the range of the neck when playing changes

- To understand how to build creative licks from the arpeggio

C Major 7

Cmaj7 will be our workhorse arpeggio and is spelled C (root), E (3rd), G (5th), B (7th).

We'll learn all the arpeggio shapes in this chapter from root notes on the sixth and fifth strings. All the shapes will be two-octave patterns, which will take care of the shapes with root notes on the fourth and third strings.

First, we'll look at the standard "box position" shapes that are typically arranged in a four- or five-fret zone on the neck.

Here's the sixth string root shape for Cmaj7 covering two octaves, ascending and descending.

Example 1a

Next, the fifth string root box position shape. Notice that I jump outside the box to play the final B.

Example 1b

These major 7 shapes are useful when we're playing a jazz standard where the chord changes are located close together on the neck and we want to work in one small zone (e.g., over a progression such as Cmaj7 – F9 – Em7). But often, you'll need to move between positions on the fretboard, and for this you need an extended arpeggio shape that uses more of the range of the neck.

Here is the sixth string root Cmaj7 arpeggio in extended form. Given the pattern of this shape, it makes sense to continue it and add more notes on the first string.

Example 1c

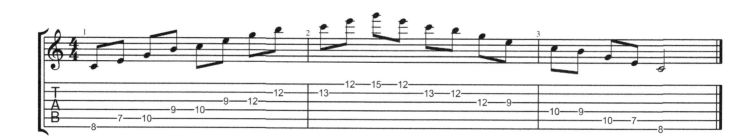

Here is the extended pattern for the fifth string root arpeggio.

Example 1d

There is another useful way to play these arpeggios, favoured by players such as Tim Miller and Greg Howe. "212" arpeggio shapes lend themselves to playing quicker, legato-style arpeggio runs.

They are so named because they follow a predictable pattern of two notes on one string, one note on the next, two notes on the next, and so on.

At first, it may seem like you're making unnecessary stretches to play these shapes, but if you persevere, you might just fall in love with them. I like to use them myself, as the shapes fall under the fingers and it definitely feels like you are flowing across the strings more easily once you get used to them.

Here is the 212 shape for the sixth string root arpeggio, ascending and descending. We'll bend the 212 rule slightly with this first pattern and extend the arpeggio to include the high E note on the first string, 12th fret. We'll also add a low B note to the end of the shape on the descent, which makes for a more pleasing, musical line to play.

Example 1e

And now the fifth string root shape.

Example 1f

Arpeggio connections

Now that we have three different ways of playing the major 7 arpeggio, the next step is to make *arpeggio connections* by linking together these shapes. This will help us in our goal to play arpeggios using the full range of the neck. The extended arpeggio patterns we've learned will help us to move seamlessly between zones on the neck.

The following exercise links the fifth string root extended arpeggio with the sixth string root box position arpeggio.

Example 1g

Next, a more ambitious line that combines both of the 212 arpeggio shapes. To play this smoothly requires a fast, first finger slide on the first string to move position.

Play the arpeggio as normal until your first finger frets the G note on the first string, 3rd fret. Quickly slide up to the 7th fret and pause very fractionally before sliding up one more fret. Now you're in position to play the descending shape.

Example 1h

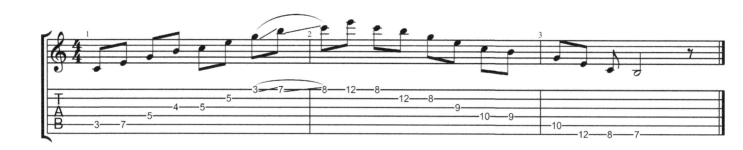

The next example connects together parts of three different shapes to cover a wide range of the neck. Play through this slowly and focus on playing each note evenly, making smooth position changes as you ascend.

Example 1i

Now, reverse this pattern and play it descending. This is trickier than it sounds, because you'll find it requires different fingering on the way down. Work out a fingering that feels comfortable to you and executes the line efficiently. Practice it slowly and embed the pattern into muscle memory.

Example 1j

For a further challenge, let's drill this whole pattern, ascending and descending. The result is a beautiful sounding line that rises and falls as it ascends. It's quite tricky to play cleanly, so focus on getting the fingering changes sounding smooth.

Example 1k

Avoiding the root

So far, we've played the major 7 arpeggio shapes from the root note every time. This is a great way to learn them initially, because the root gives us a strong "home" position on the neck to which we can return and know exactly where we are.

In real musical situations, however, we often want to avoid the root and "disguise" our arpeggios to make them sound less obvious. If we play every arpeggio from the root over a set of chord changes, it will sound like "playing by numbers" and we want to be more creative than that.

The remedy is to build lines that start from the other Cmaj7 chord tones, apart from the C root (E, G, B). They can end on any of the four chord tones, but we want to avoid the root at the beginning.

To begin, here are three examples that start on the 3rd (E). Notice that they sound more like melodic lines we might play and less like arpeggio patterns.

This first example also ends on the 3rd.

Example 1l

This extended line ends on the 7th. At the end of bar one, play the first string 7th fret with your first finger then slide up one fret to play the 8th also with the first finger. Play the 12th fret with the fourth finger.

Example 1m

This line ends on the 7th too. This time you'll execute a descending first string slide with the first finger.

Example 1n

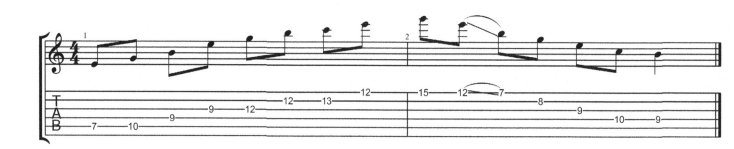

Now let's look at some arpeggio lines built from the 5th (G). Here's an idea that begins on G, ends on B, and includes a legato slide.

Example 1o

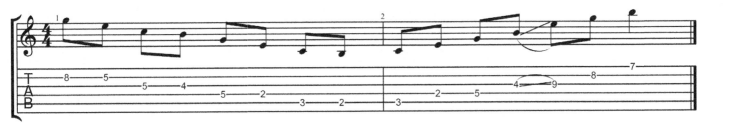

This idea begins and ends on G. Look out for the tricky position shift here. I find it easier to play a legato slide to move from the 8th to the 12th fret of the first string, which puts you in the right position to play the rest of the line.

Example 1p

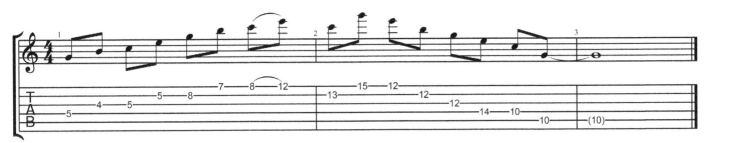

Now for a few lines that begin on the 7th (B). Arpeggios built from the 7th can sound very beautiful and melodic. It's worth noting that since the 7th is only a half step away from the root (B to C), launching an arpeggio line from the 7th can sound like we're using a chromatic approach note – a very common idea in jazz. Below is a simple take on our fifth string root extended arpeggio, starting and ending on B.

Example 1q

This falling and rising line begins on B and ends on E.

Example 1r

This example plays a similar phrase each time it descends, but in a different part of the fretboard, which alters the timbre.

Example 1s

So far, we've played the arpeggio in a fairly linear manner, but we can also mix up the sequence and play wider intervallic jumps. Here's a line that rapidly ascends the fretboard, repeating certain arpeggio notes to facilitate the interval jumps.

Example 1t

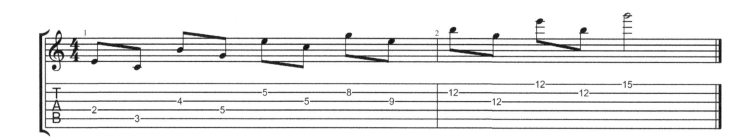

Here are a couple more string skipping/interval skipping ideas.

Example 1u

Example 1v

Finally, this idea takes advantage of the places on the fretboard where arpeggio notes can be played in perfect 4ths.

Example 1w

We could spend more time drilling the arpeggio to create further sequencing ideas, but this is something you can do in your practice sessions with the shapes from the beginning of the chapter. Instead, let's look at how to use the arpeggio to create some authentic jazz vocabulary.

Targeting arpeggio tones with passing notes

Now that you have a good grasp of the fretboard geography of the Cmaj7 arpeggio, it's time to get more creative. The addition of passing notes will enable us to play authentic sounding arpeggio-driven jazz licks.

Jazz is all about tension and release – momentarily playing outside the key, then coming back inside. One of the best/ easiest ways to achieve this is to use an arpeggio as the framework for a lick and approach the chord tones chromatically from above or below. It's a tried and tested formula that provided the vocabulary used by all the great jazz guitarists down the years.

In this section I'll show you how transform an arpeggio shape into a melodic lick. For the first few examples, I'll show exactly which shape from earlier in the chapter I had in mind when composing the lick. Once you understand the concept, later you can explore this idea on your own.

In Example 1d we played an extended arpeggio shape with its root on the fifth string. Here I've taken a fragment of that shape using just the notes on the top four strings.

Shape 1

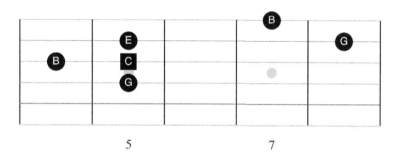

We can turn this shape into a lick by approaching the arpeggio tones with passing notes. Think of this process as *targeting* the arpeggio tones. There are several ways in which we can do this, but first, fix this idea in your mind:

The arpeggio shape spans five frets. All the other notes on the top four strings in that five-fret zone are potential passing notes. Nearly all of them can be used to create melodic lines if you follow this simple rule:

Play arpeggio notes mostly on downbeats and passing notes mostly on upbeats.

As long as you stick to this rule, your licks will sound grounded. You can take liberties with passing notes, even if they sound quite outside, as long as you hit an arpeggio note on the beat most of the time, because this will keep your listeners connected with the harmony.

This first example uses two passing notes on the second string. They fill the gap between the G and E arpeggio notes.

Example 1x

This line descends the Cmaj7 arpeggio from the 7th (B) to root, then uses passing notes that target the 7th an octave lower.

Example 1y

Placing a passing note below the 3rd (E) of a major 7 arpeggio immediately gives a lick a bluesy feel.

Example 1z

This line emphasises the jazz-blues feel even more by focusing longer on the b3 to 3rd movement.

Example 1z1

Here's one more line using this shape featuring a passing note descending run.

Example 1z2

Now let's extend our arpeggio shape to its full two-octaves and turn it into a passing note lick.

Shape 2

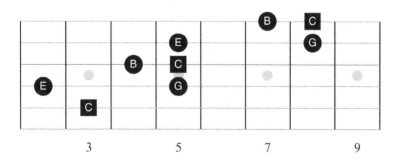

Example 1z3 is a lick built around this shape. It might look complex at first but let me break it down for you bar by bar, so you can see exactly how each part is constructed.

At the beginning of the lick, we target the B arpeggio note on the third string, 4th fret. This is done by playing a passing note a half step above it, then walking up to it chromatically from the 2nd fret. The B arpeggio tone lands right on beat 1. This simple four-note idea is an absolute staple of bebop phrasing.

Next comes a G arpeggio note, then a passing A note borrowed from the opening phrase. Then we have a passing note which resolves to an arpeggio note from a half step above (F to E). Bar one is completed by a root, 7th, root movement.

Play only the pickup bar and bar one now. Visualise how the passing notes work around the simple arpeggio structure.

From here on, the arpeggio is less disguised. Bar two is almost straight arpeggio notes, but two passing notes are added on the second string.

In bar three, the first five notes are all arpeggio tones. The lick ends by mirroring the chromatic ascending line of bar two an octave lower.

Take a moment to visualise the arpeggio shape, now play through the whole line.

Example 1z3

Here is another line built on this same shape.

Example 1z4

Now let's try our original box shape arpeggio from Example 1a. Here's a reminder of how it's laid out.

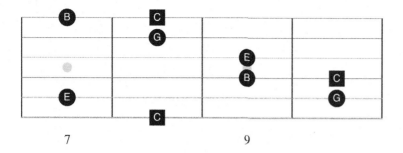

Below is a passing note line built around this shape.

Example 1z5

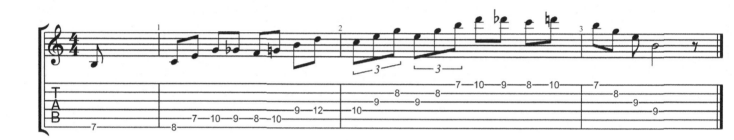

Remember that the arpeggio tones are your anchor points and you can play almost anything around them as long as you hit arpeggio tones on down beats *most of the time*. It's not an immovable rule, but if you play passing notes on the beat all the time, your audience will soon lose track of the harmony.

Now that you've seen several lines created using arpeggio shapes, you can practice this on your own. Take a box or extended shape and begin to work with it, approaching the arpeggio tones from below and above. Be sure to listen to some of the great bebop guitar players, like Pat Martino, who use this idea in their playing all the time.

To close out this chapter, here are a few more licks to check out. See if you can identify the arpeggio shapes I had in mind when playing them.

Next we have a tried and trusted bebop lick that weaves around the arpeggio tones. The Bb passing note is so useful in this context for connecting to the C root note via the 7th.

Example 1z6

Here's a faster 1/16th note bebop lick. In bar two, you'll easily spot the Cmaj7 arpeggio shape. From there, the arpeggio descends in a sequence as it moves into the lower register.

Example 1z7

Next, an 1/8th note lick that ends on the 3rd of Cmaj7.

Example 1z8

The next lick begins with string skips through the arpeggio before a short passing note phrase. In bar two, we ascend the arpeggio in the first half. In the second half, the final four notes are a simple *displacement* or "sidestep" idea. The first two notes of this phrase are both passing note (A, F). They belong to the C Major parent scale and are the 6th and 4th degree respectively. The next two notes are the same phrase lowered a half step. The G# is the chromatic #5 passing note, then we resolve to an E arpeggio tone (the 3rd of Cmaj7).

Example 1z9

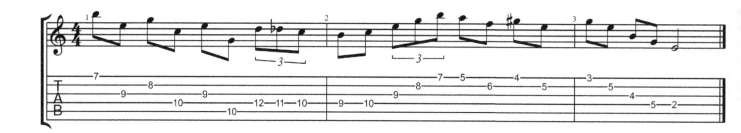

To end this chapter, here's an idea that Joe Pass often used in his playing: enclosing arpeggio tones with notes above and below the target. Look at bar one and notice that the second note in each four-note group is a Cmaj7 arpeggio tone. They spell out C, E, G, B.

The notes that enclose the arpeggio tones can come from either the C Major parent scale or be chromatic notes from outside the key. It can be a matter of taste whether a scale tone enclosure or a chromatic enclosure sounds "right" in the context of a piece of music, so use your ears and discretion when experimenting with this idea.

The enclosure idea continues until beat 4 of bar two where we transition into a more traditional bebop lick.

Example 1z10

NB: In the appendix to this book, I've included "arpeggio maps" for each chord. These visual maps show you how each arpeggio is distributed across the fretboard, from frets 1-17. You'll find them useful to refer to when you want to compose your own arpeggio-based licks.

Chapter Two – Minor 9 Arpeggios

Minor 9 chords

Now we turn our attention to minor chords. In this book, my aim is to teach you the most useful arpeggios for the jazz guitarist – the arpeggios used by the great players when soloing over standards. The minor 9 is a sound that is frequently used, and this extra note goes a long way to creating authentic sounding jazz vocabulary. In this chapter I'll also show you a neat trick you can apply to minor 9 arpeggios to instantly create some cool sounding lines.

The minor 9 often functions as the ii chord in the ii V I sequence (Dm9 – G7 – Cmaj7 in the key of C Major). Minor 9 arpeggios are useful to spell out the ii chord in that context, but are also essential for playing on modal jazz tunes (which often feature multiple bars of minor chords) and for soloing over the i chord in a minor ii V I (Bm7b5 – E7#5 – Am9, for example).

Here's a reminder of our goals for working with this arpeggio:

* To learn the arpeggio in several different locations on the neck

* To learn it in a way that will enable us to make better fretboard connections and use more of the range of the neck when playing changes

* To understand how to build creative licks from the arpeggio

D minor 9

Dm9 is spelled D (root), F (b3), A (5th), C (b7), E (9th). Because of the way the intervals fall on the fretboard, we don't need the 212 shapes used in the previous chapter and will instead focus on box position and extended shapes.

First, here is the Dm9 box arpeggio shape with the root on the sixth string. With this shape, we can play two octaves and three notes from a third octave.

Example 2a

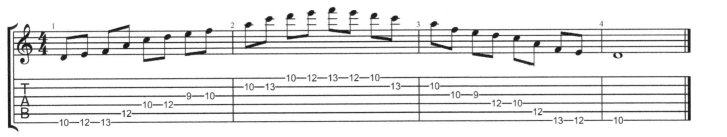

Next, the 5th string box shape. Notice that the addition of the 9th interval makes these patterns sound more like lines than straight arpeggios.

Example 2b

Because the Dm9 arpeggio is located towards the middle of the neck, there is an alternative fifth string root shape we can play in the lower region. To complete two octaves, however, we need to break out of the box, so this becomes our first extended arpeggio shape.

Example 2c

The 6th string root extended arpeggio shape spans ten frets and starts high up the neck. If you're playing an archtop and the 20th fret feels somewhat inaccessible, you can omit the high C note.

Example 2d

If we play an extended arpeggio shape from the root on the fifth string, due to the interval layout we have a couple of possible options. Here's the first:

Example 2e

Now try this alternative rapidly ascending shape. It requires several quick position changes which you can execute by jumping your fretting hand forward or via a slide. It's an effective shape for quickly spanning a wide range of the neck.

Example 2f

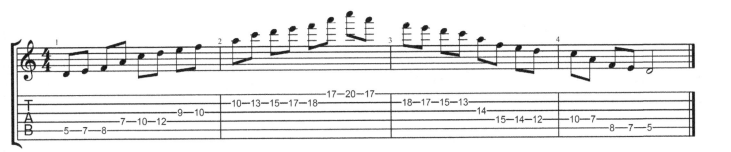

Spend a decent amount of time drilling these core arpeggio shapes, because they form the bedrock of the melodic ideas that are to come. The more fluent you are with the arpeggio shapes, the easier you'll find it to create convincing jazz licks of your own. Try to commit them to memory.

Arpeggio connections

Now it's time to move on to making *arpeggio connections* by linking together these patterns across the fretboard. Each pattern will begin on a root note, but this time we're not concerned about playing the intervals of the arpeggio in order – we're focusing on moving in and out of the patterns across the fretboard.

Example 2g begins in the lower position shown in Example 2c and climbs to the high position box shape.

Example 2g

Here's a way of descending through the shapes beginning at the 12th fret of the first string and descending all the way down to the open A string (the 5th of Dm9).

Example 2h

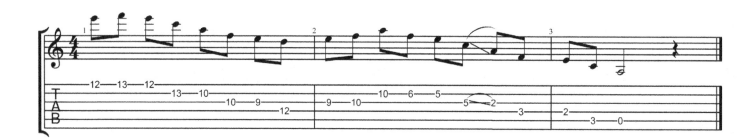

This connected line begins in fifth position and uses two legato slides to shift position into the 10th position box shape.

Example 2i

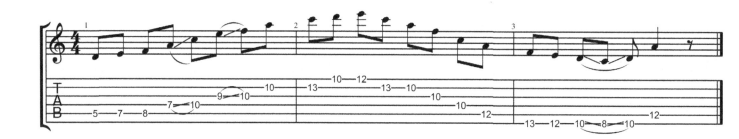

This line traverses the neck from the sixth string root note down to an open first string. It ends on the 5th.

Example 2j

Finally, here is a longer line that ebbs and flows. In bar three, slide from the 12th to 13th fret with the first finger and you should be able to reach the high A note at the 17th with the fourth finger. This connected line ends on the 9th (E).

Example 2k

Avoiding the root

To make our arpeggios sound more musical, we want to develop the skill of being able to visualise the arpeggio patterns but not playing them from the root every time. Here are some arpeggio patterns built from the other Dm9 chord tones. First, a couple of lines that begin on the b3 (F).

This first example begins in the lower register and uses a legato slide to move into the mid-neck position. It starts and ends with the same phrase that pedals between the b3 and 9th.

Example 2l

The next lick uses the simple idea of a repeating motif to descend from a high to low F. It doesn't use the D root note and works well as a lick on its own.

Example 2m

Here's one more line that begins on the b3, this time ending on the 9th. You can alternate pick this line, but it lends itself to being played legato, as indicated below.

Example 2n

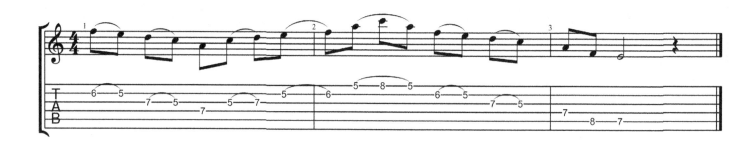

Now let's explore some arpeggio lines that begin on the 5th (A) of Dm9.

This first idea takes advantage of the fifth position box shape Dm9 arpeggio.

Example 2o

The next example uses mostly the sixth string root box shape and begins and ends on the 5th.

Example 2p

Example 2q is a descending line that begins and ends on the 5th.

Example 2q

The next group of examples are arpeggio lines built from the b7 (C).

I've included fingering suggestions for the first part of Example 2r, as the opening ascending phrase can be tricky to play smoothly. This line begins and ends on the b7. Using the b7 in this way can create a subtle tension, because although it's a chord tone, the C really wants to resolve to D.

Example 2r

Here is a very simple but effective line that works as a lick in its own right, descending from b7 to b7.

Example 2s

This is a descending line that uses some legato slides to change position.

Example 2t

The final set of examples in this section all begin on the 9th (E) interval. This first lick is a simple one, but an absolute staple of jazz guitar vocabulary you'll have heard before.

Example 2u

The next line makes a jump between the mid and high arpeggio shapes. Play the A note at the end of bar one with your first finger, then either slide it up to the tenth or quickly jump up to it.

Example 2v

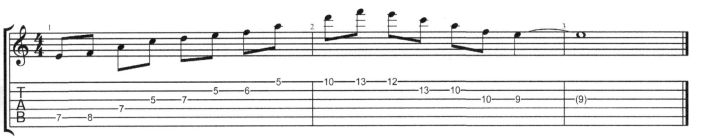

Lastly, here is a pedal tone idea that begins and ends on the 9th.

Example 2w

A trick with the 9th

A simple trick you can apply to the minor 9 arpeggio is to omit the b7 and return in to a four-note structure. This approach is commonly used by modern jazz guitar players to create a more ambiguous, ethereal sound. The next group of lines will be constructed using the notes D (root), F (b3), A (5th), E (9th). These lines also include some more intervallic and string skipping ideas.

The first example is an ascending line that launches from the root note and ends on the 9th. You can hear that the omission of the b7 immediately creates a more spacious sound.

Example 2x

Example 2y is a string skipping intervallic line that begins and ends on the D root.

Example 2y

Next, a modern sounding jazz line that utilises the open first string to make a quick position change.

Example 2z

Here's one final 1 b3 5 9 idea that begins with some large intervallic jumps. It demands some fretting hand dexterity to switch positions, so work through it slowly and decide on an economical fingering that feels comfortable to you.

Example 2z1

Targeting arpeggio tones with passing notes

I hope you'll agree that the addition of the 9th to the basic minor 7 arpeggio is, in itself, a useful tool that can produce some great melodic results. Now that we have thoroughly explored the sound and shape of the minor 9, we can take things a step further and use it to create some authentic sounding jazz licks with the addition of passing notes. Here are ten licks built around the shapes you've learned in this chapter, which use passing notes to target the arpeggio tones.

The first example begins with an approach note from a half step below. This C# note is used again in bar three. It can be viewed as a note borrowed from the D Melodic Minor scale, and always evokes that characteristic melodic minor tension.

Example 2z2

Passing notes occur throughout this next lick to target the arpeggio tones. In bar two, the first two notes are non-arpeggio tones (B, G) then this two-note phrase is moved down a whole step to play the 5th (A) and b3 (F) of D minor, followed by the 9th (E).

In bar three, the intervallic phrase allows a C# passing note to fall on the down beat. C# is the major 7, rather than the b7 (C) arpeggio tone, and implies a Dmin(Maj7) sound that hints at the melodic minor.

Example 2z3

In this example, the passing notes are used to create a cascading descending run.

Example 2z4

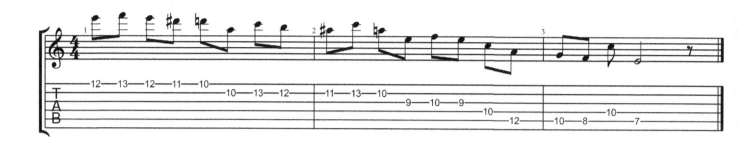

Next is a must-know bebop staple lick. It begins with a passing note that targets the 5th of D minor.

Example 2z5

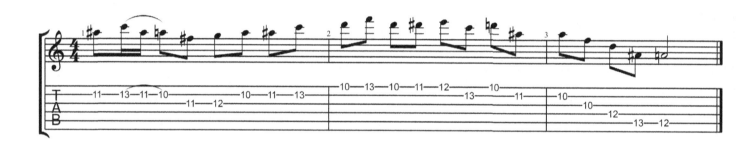

In bar one of this example, start with the fretting hand in 5th position and move to 7th position for the notes on the fourth string. You can execute the slide from 10th to 12th fret with the third or fourth finger, whichever feels most comfortable.

Example 2z6

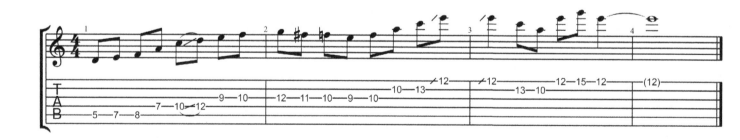

This melodic line is constructed around the sixth string root Dm9 arpeggio shape.

Example 2z7

The C# note is working hard again in this lick. It's such a useful passing note as the sound of targeting the root from a half step below is so prevalent in bebop.

Example 2z8

For this example, begin with your fretting hand anchored at 5th position for bars 1-2, then quickly switch to 2nd position for bar three.

Example 2z9

The final three examples of this chapter feature longer lines. They represent the kind of ideas you can play over a longer D minor vamp (such as in the tunes *So What* and *Impressions*).

The phrase that spans bar one to halfway through bar three is an "enclosure" idea (i.e. arpeggio notes are surrounded by other notes). Arpeggio tones fall on the off beats here, and are surrounded by either parent scale notes or passing notes above and below.

For the long chromatic run down on the first string in the second half of bar three, use one-finger-per-string fretting, starting with the fourth finger on the 13th. To continue the run down at the beginning of bar four, execute a quick fretting hand position shift and play the 9th fret with the fourth finger again. It can take a bit of practice to get the descent sounding smooth.

Example 2z10

Example 2z11 starts cool and laid back but launches into a 1/16th note run for bar two.

Example 2z11

Finally, here's a swinging bebop-style lick to close out this chapter. The focus of the opening run is to target the B note on the first string. This non-arpeggio tone is 6th/13th of D minor. Played in this higher register, it implies that the underlying chord is Dm13.

The phrase in bar three is similar, this time targeting the 9th.

Example 2z12

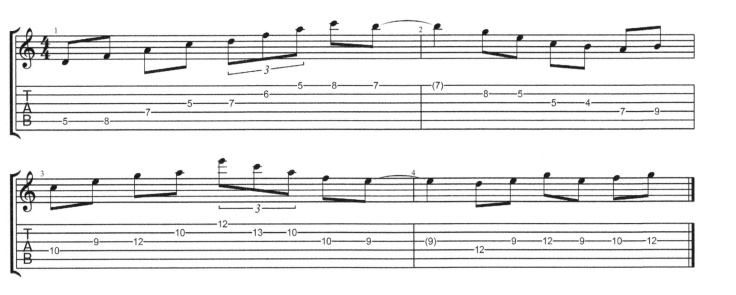

Chapter Three – Dominant 7b9 Arpeggios

Dominant 7b9 chords

In this chapter we're going to look at the dominant 7 arpeggio. Combined with the work done in previous chapters, if you master this arpeggio, you'll have vocabulary to play on each chord in the major ii V I sequence. By the end of this book we'll have combined both major and minor ii V Is, and you'll be equipped to play over the most common sequences in jazz harmony.

Again, we could have studied a straight dominant 7, but it makes more sense to extend the arpeggio with the addition of the b9. The dominant 7b9 is *the sound* of bebop in a nutshell. Charlie Parker used it extensively in his playing and it became deeply embedded in the sound of modern jazz.

The b9 is perhaps the most widely used method of resolving the dominant V chord to the tonic, with its descending half step movement. It's incredibly useful to study because it works in either a major or minor ii V I context. E.g.:

Dm9 – G7b9 – Cmaj7

Or,

Bm7b5 – E7b9 – Am9

In both cases, the b9 note resolves down a half step to the 5th of the I chord.

G7b9

G7b9 is spelled G (root), B (3rd), D (5th), F (b7), Ab (b9). Let's look at the common box position shapes for this arpeggio. First, the sixth string root shape.

Because of the layout of this arpeggio on the fretboard, we have options when it comes to the box positions. Example 3a shows a pattern that utilises consecutive notes on each string, so that the root and b9 are played one after the other.

Example 3a

Then we have two alternative "121" shapes (the opposite of the 212 shapes from Chapter One i.e. one note per string, two notes per string, one note per sting, etc.)

Here's the first, which uses the frets below the root position.

Example 3b

And the alternative, which uses frets above the root position.

Example 3c

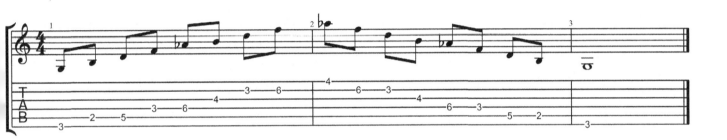

We'll approach the 5th string box shapes in the same way. First, the shape that uses consecutive notes on each string. With this shape, it's normal to ascend to, and descend from, the F note at the 13th fret.

Example 3d

Then we have a "121" shape (though it's common to cheat and add in that high F again).

Example 3e

And, finally, an alternative shape from the 5th string root that just falls nicely on the fretboard.

Example 3f

Now let's move on to look at some extended patterns for the 7b9 that use more of the range of the fretboard, beginning with the sixth string root.

This first pattern uses the consecutive note idea of Example 3a.

Example 3g

The layout of this arpeggio means there are a few possible transition points (the point at which you need to change string to continue ascending), so here is a slightly different approach.

Example 3h

Now play this extended fifth string root shape, ascending and descending.

Example 3i

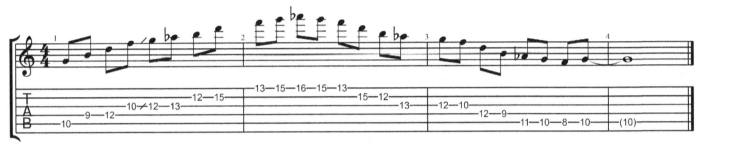

Example 3j shows a different route we can take to reach the higher register.

Example 3j

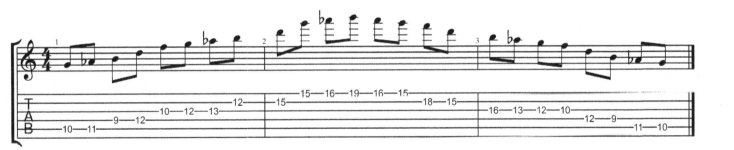

Arpeggio connections

Next, we'll continue to drill this arpeggio by making some *connections* across the fretboard. We'll start each line from the G root note, but our aim is to explore different melodic patterns on the fretboard, without being too concerned about the order of the notes. This will further reinforce the sound of the arpeggio in our ears.

This first example covers a wide range of the fretboard and ends on the b9.

Example 3k

This arpeggio connection snakes across the fretboard from 5th position into the higher zone of the neck.

Example 3l

Next, a connection that begins in 10th position with the simplified fifth string root shape, then works its way back down the fretboard.

Example 3m

Here's one more connection.

Example 3n

Avoiding the root

Hopefully, the previous exercises have begun to embed the sound of the 7b9 arpeggio in your ears, and you're getting to grips with its fretboard geography. Next, we will work through a collection of melodic lines that avoid beginning on the G root note.

First, some lines built from the 3rd (B).

This line begins on the 3rd and resolves to the root.

Example 3o

Here is a modern, angular sounding line. The dominant 7b9 chord has a close connection with the diminished scale and you may recognise the first four notes of bar one as spelling a diminished 7 chord.

Example 3p

The next example begins and ends on the 3rd and really exploits the "diminished connection" of the 7b9. To play this line, hold down the four-note diminished 7 chord shape on the top four strings and move it up the neck. In bar three we break away from that pattern to end the line.

Example 3q

The next few examples play the arpeggio from the 5th (D).

First, here's a way of ascending the fretboard, launching from 5th position.

Example 3r

The next example takes the opposite approach and descends, beginning and ending on the 5th.

Example 3s

Finally, this line ascends in a geometric fashion, repeating the same phrase with small modifications to the shape being played.

Example 3t

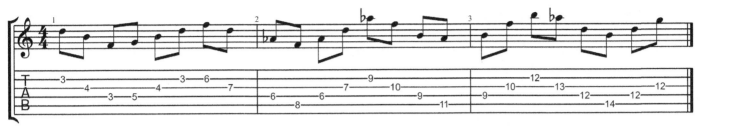

Next, we move on to explore some lines played from the b7 (F) of G7b9.

This is a simple but effective way of outlining the sound of the arpeggio.

Example 3u

Here's a line that begins and ends on the b7.

Example 3v

The next example hints at the diminished/7b9 connection again as it descends from a high F to the open G string.

Example 3w

And lastly, some lines played from the b9 (Ab).

To begin with, a simple line that outlines the sound of the arpeggio from b9 to 5th.

Example 3x

Here's a similar approach using the lower register.

Example 3y

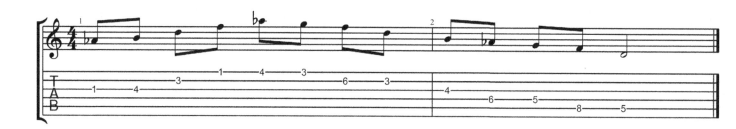

Finally, we have a line that really captures the diminished flavour of the 7b9. It's organised into 1/8th note triplets moving in minor thirds.

Example 3z

Targeting arpeggio tones with passing notes

This arpeggio doesn't need too much persuasion to sound outside, and we want to be sure to highlight the b9 interval in our lines, so many of the passing note ideas here are about placing approach notes above or below the other chord tones.

To kick things off, this first lick approaches the G root note from a half step below. On beat 2 of bar one, the four-note phrase encloses the G root with the b9 (Ab) above and an F# approach note below.

Example 3z1

This lick mixes up 1/8th note triplets with straight 1/8ths and 1/16ths to create a rhythmically interesting line.

Example 3z2

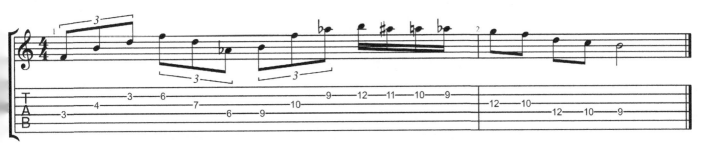

As soon as we begin to add chromatic passing notes around the chord tones of G7b9 we inevitably hit upon other alterations of the dominant chord, functioning as approach notes, such as the #5 (D#) at the end of bar one that targets the D.

Example 3z3

This lick uses the #5 again to approach the 5th (D) from above, and in bar two, the #9 (A#) to approach the 3rd (B) from below.

Example 3z4

The next example starts off with a regular ascent of the arpeggio from the sixth string root, then from the "3&" of bar one places approach notes from above in front of chord tones. The line breaks out of this pattern at the end of bar two.

Example 3z5

This lick weaves around the chord tones much more, but still retains the sound of the arpeggio.

Example 3z6

Next is an 1/8th note triplet-driven line that uses pull-offs on the first string to descend arpeggio tones. This lick calls for some quick fretting hand position shifts, so practice the movements you're going to make slowly before bringing this up to tempo.

Example 3z7

Example 3z8 is a more swinging bebop style lick.

Example 3z8

This more modern sounding lick, beginning on the b9, contrasts the previous idea. Bar one features #11 (C#) and #9 (A#) passing notes to ratchet up the tension. The lick descends to a strong root note resolution in bar two.

Example 3z9

The last example is an 1/8th note triplet line that works through a series of chord tones pairing them with chromatic notes a half step below. On beat 2 of bar two, we break out of this pattern to highlight the b9 tonality with a diminished run and the line ends on the G root.

Example 3z10

Chapter Four – Minor 7b5 Arpeggios

Minor 7b5 chords

We are working towards mastering the arpeggios that make up the major and minor ii V I sequences in jazz, and next we're looking at the minor 7b5 chord, also known as the half-diminished.

This is the ii chord in the minor ii V i progression, and we'll use Bm7b5 as our model. It belongs to the *relative minor* sequence of the major sequence we've been studying (C Major / A Minor). i.e.

Major ii V I = Dm7 – G7 – Cmaj7

Minor ii V i = Bm7b5 – E7 – Am7

Combine these sequences and you have the basis of the *Autumn Leaves* progression.

The minor 7b5 chord can sound quite dissonant and unresolved when played in isolation, but it comes into its own as part of the minor ii V i, where it usually leads to an altered dominant chord. In this context, it works wonderfully well.

Bm7b5

Bm7b5 is spelled B (root), D (b3), F (b5), A (b7)

Although this chord has only one note different to Bm7, the b5 interval makes all the difference when it comes to how the arpeggio is distributed across the fretboard and the kind of melodic lines we can create from it.

We'll begin by looking at the commonly played box arpeggio shapes. First, the sixth string root shape.

Example 4a

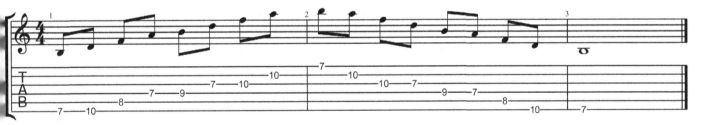

And now the fifth string root shape.

Example 4b

There are also some "212" shape variations for this arpeggio. It's definitely worth practicing these, because they really come into their own with this chord and make the arpeggio much more easily playable.

Here's how to play the sixth string root shape. This shape eliminates the awkward parallel notes at the 10th fret of the box shape that are played with the fourth finger. Although there is more of a stretch on the second string, it's worth doing because the arpeggio flows much better across the strings.

Example 4c

Next we have the equivalent fifth string root 212 pattern. The same can be said of this variation: it's more of a stretch, but less of a position change, so the arpeggio can be played more smoothly. If you find the stretch too much, do a quick "hand throw" (moving the hand quickly forward then back while playing the notes on the first string). You only need to move your hand very slightly to make fretting the notes easier.

Example 4d

Next, we'll look at some patterns for extending this arpeggio to use more of the range of the neck.

First, the extended pattern from the fifth string root. This approach may suit you if you're comfortable making reasonably big stretches and it's quite an economical pattern with two notes on each string. Use hand throws to move smoothly between positions.

Example 4e

Here's an alternative way to play the same extended shape if you prefer smaller stretches.

Example 4f

Next, here is the extended shape with the root on the sixth string. The stretches are easily achievable in this zone of the neck.

Example 4g

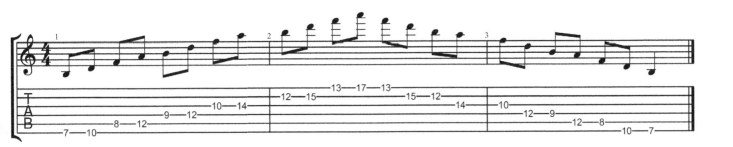

The next example is an alternative extended shape for the sixth string root that omits the high A note.

Example 4h

Arpeggio connections

Now it's time to find some arpeggio connections across the fretboard. Remember that although we'll begin each pattern on a root note, we're not concerned about playing the intervals in order – it's all about learning the fretboard geography of the arpeggio.

Here's a simple connected arpeggio that ascends from the fifth string root in interval order, then descends from the A note on the first string, 5th fret, landing on the B root at the end.

Example 4i

This line connects the upper notes of the sixth string root box shape with the fifth string root extended shape, doubling back on certain notes to form a melodic pattern.

Example 4j

The next arpeggio line begins by ascending the sixth string root shape from Example 4a, but then transitions down the fretboard, looking for connections that will resolve the line to the fifth string shape.

Example 4k

This example begins in the upper octave of the fifth position extended shape. The rest of the line spells out two common Bm7b5 chord shapes you may recognise.

Example 4l

Avoiding the root

In the next dozen examples, we're going to play minor 7b5 lines that avoid the root note of the chord, launching from the b3, b5 and b7 respectively. These immediately sound more like licks than arpeggio patterns and the sound we're spelling out is less obvious. In your practice sessions, work at visualising an arpeggio shape on the fretboard, then find every way possible to play lines around it without starting from the root.

Here are some lines played from the b3 (D).

The first line begins and ends on the b3

Example 4m

This line works as a descending run from a high D.

Example 4n

This line, which begins on the b3 and ends on the root, has the ideal shape for playing a faster legato run to add some variety to your lines.

Example 4o

Now, from the b5 (F).

Here's a way of playing the arpeggio from b5 to b5. I've added fingering directions to the notation for this example. This is my recommendation to navigate the notes that fall on the same fret on adjacent strings.

Example 4p

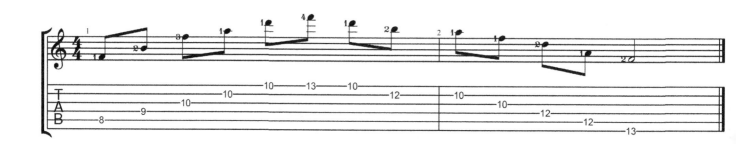

Next, another b5 to b5 idea.

Example 4q

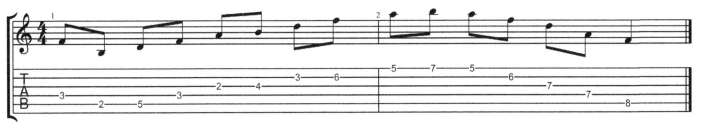

Here's a simple but effective route through the arpeggio that uses a repeating two-string pattern.

Example 4r

Lastly, here are some lines built from the b7 (A).

To begin with, a line that works well as a short lick from b7 to b7.

Example 4s

Next, a line running from the b7 to the root note that has an almost pentatonic feel to it, due to the note arrangement on each string.

Example 4t

And here's a way of playing the arpeggio from b7 to b5, all within 7th position.

Example 4u

Targeting arpeggio tones with passing notes

Next we're going to get even more musical with this arpeggio and explore some lines created with the addition of passing notes. With an arpeggio like the minor 7b5 it's important to highlight the tones that give it its unique character (especially the b3 and b5 combination), so that we don't obscure its identity. But that doesn't mean we can't use carefully placed chromatic approach notes to spice up our lines.

To kick things off, here's an ascending sequenced idea. Bars 1-2 contain only arpeggio notes. In bar three, beat 2, a half step approach note targets the b5, then a chromatic descending run targets the root.

Example 4v

This lick is built around the 7th position box shape. It adds C# approach notes before each b3 (D), and a G# before the b7 (A).

Example 4w

This is another line built around the same shape, but with more passing notes. Each chromatic note adds its own kind of tension when superimposed over Bm7b5.

Example 4x

Example 4y

This line leads with a passing note that targets the b5 (F) from a half step below twice in bar one. In bar two, use downwards slides for the position shifts in the descending run.

Example 4z

This lick begins by spelling out a common Bm7b5 voicing in 9th position with the first four notes. This is followed by a bebop displacement trick. Two arpeggio notes are played (B, A), then played a half step below (A#, G#), then the G# resolves back to A.

Example 4z1

This line follows a pattern that repeats up the octave before breaking out to end on the b5 (F).

Example 4z2

Here's an easy but effective way of spelling the sound of Bm7b5 leading with two chromatic descending runs.

Example 4z3

This line contains several passing notes. From the middle of bar two, all four Bm7b5 chord tones are preceded by a note a half step below.

Example 4z4

The next line mixes 1/8th note triplets with straight 1/16th notes for rhythmic surprise. The C passing note anticipates the B root note from a half step above to end.

Example 4z5

Next, try this fast 1/16th note run. Use hammer-ons for the two-note-per-string ascending run. You'll end this run with your second finger fretting the 12th fret, second string. Quickly shift your hand to 7th position, with your fourth finger fretting the 10th fret, first string, for the chromatic run down. Drill the lick slowly and get your position shifts in place before bringing it up to tempo.

Example 4z6

Finally, we have a descending line that uses passing notes to weave around the arpeggio tones. At the end of bar one you'll be fretting the fourth string, 12th fret, with your third finger. Quickly jump the third finger over to the second string to begin the phrase in bar two.

Example 4z7

Chapter Five –7#5b9 Arpeggios

Dominant 7#5b9 chords

In the previous chapter we worked with the minor 7b5 arpeggio – chord ii in the minor ii V i progression. In this chapter we turn our attention to the V chord in this sequence. In the minor ii V i this is usually some sort of altered dominant chord. E.g. Bm7b5 – E7alt – Am7.

We already covered the 7b9 altered dominant chord in Chapter Three, but in that context the 7b9 arpeggio was chosen for its suitability in the major ii V I.

The 7b9 can also work well in a minor ii V i, but in this sequence it's normal to include more than one altered tension.

We could go nuts with altered tensions here, but remember the focus of this book is to explore the *most useful* sounds commonly used in melodic jazz lines. For that reason, I've chosen to combine the b9 and #5 altered tensions in one arpeggio. (The more tense sounding b5 and #9 intervals are valid, of course, but tend to be less useful in bebop-orientated jazz soloing).

Our minor ii V i sequence then, will be Bm7b5 – E7#5b9 – Am9

When it comes to creating ii V i lines for this sequence in Chapter Seven, we'll use material from the minor 9 chapter to compose licks over the A minor chord – we don't need to learn anything new.

E7#5b9

E7#5b9 is spelled E (root), G# (3rd), C (#5), D (b7), F (b9)

First, let's visualise the E7#5b9 chord for a moment and hear how it sounds in the context of the minor ii V i. Here are two ways of playing the sequence:

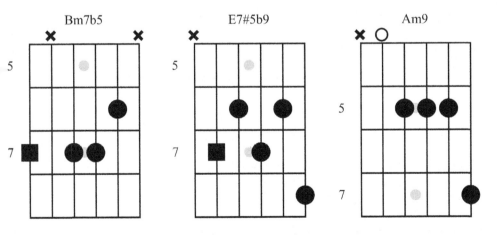

Example 5a

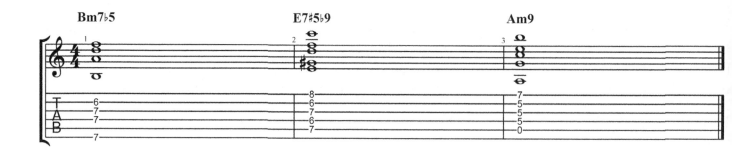

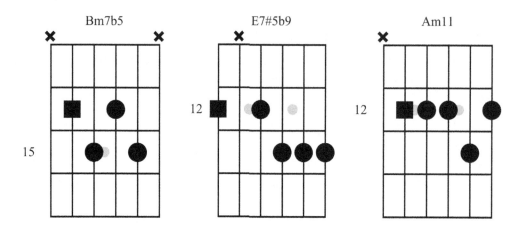

Example 5b

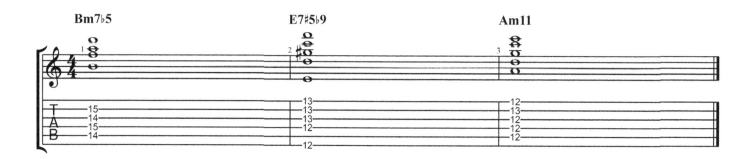

The 7#5b9 chord really enriches the progression and once we begin drilling the arpeggio and turning it into melodic lines, I think you'll discover it makes a beautiful sound.

To get familiar with the shape of it, we'll start with this 7th position box shape with the root note on the fourth string. Play one of the above E7alt chord voicings, then run the arpeggio up and down a few times to get used to the sound of it.

Example 5c

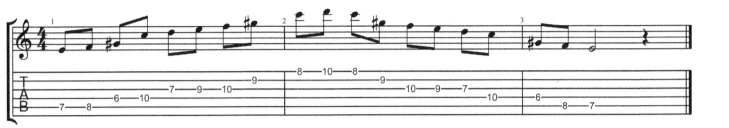

Next, here is the sixth string root box shape for E7#5b9.

Example 5d

There is another useful way to play the sixth string root shape starting in the same position but using the frets below rather than above. Instead of starting with the first finger at the 12th fret, this time use the third finger and play the 13th fret with the fourth finger.

Example 5e

Normally, our extended arpeggio shapes incorporate the fourth string root arpeggio, but since we're working with an E tonality, the fretboard layout means that it makes sense to play that shape on its own in the lower register of the neck. We can't cover two octaves in this position, but we can ascend as high as the G# note.

Example 5f

Now we can practice some extended arpeggio shapes from all three root notes that use a wider range of the neck. Let's begin with the fourth string shape from the previous example and extend it across the neck.

The geography of this arpeggio means it involves a few stretches. Play the fourth string 2nd fret with your first finger, then jump the fretting hand forward to play the 3rd fret also with the first finger.

After playing the second string 6th fret with the second finger, play the 9th fret with the fourth finger, then move into 8th position to play the first string notes with the first and second fingers.

Example 5g

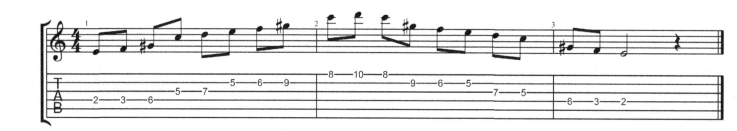

Now let's play the extended arpeggio from the fifth string root.

Example 5h

And from the 6th string root.

Example 5i

Since we're working with an E root note, we can also play an extended arpeggio from the open sixth string. This pattern combines some of the patterns we've already used into a super arpeggio spanning a wide range of the neck. You'll need to jump fretting hand position in bar two to play the 9th fret on the third string, then again on the second string to play the 13th fret.

Example 5j

Arpeggio connections

Next, we move on to a selection of arpeggio connections, linking shapes across the fretboard. We begin each connection on a root note, but we're not concerned about playing the arpeggio in interval order – we're just training our eyes and fingers to navigate the shape of the arpeggio across the fretboard.

First of all, a descending line that becomes more intervallic at the end.

Example 5k

This connection sequence is based around the fourth string root extended arpeggio pattern.

Example 5l

The next line is another descending/ascending connection.

Example 5m

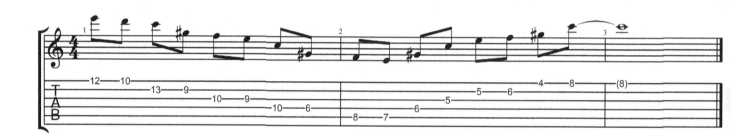

This connection begins in 7th position and returns there via a different route.

Example 5n

Avoiding the root

Next, we'll work through a collection of lines built from the other chord tones of E7#5b9, avoiding the root. This is where the arpeggio begins to sound more like music, but it can also test our ability to visualise the arpeggio pattern on the fretboard. We'll play lines from the 3rd, #5, b7 and b9. There are three examples for each.

Here are three lines built from the 3rd (G#).

This line begins on the 3rd and ends on the b9.

Example 5o

Look at the first three notes of the next line and you may recognise them as an E augmented arpeggio. It's the raised fifth interval that turns an E major triad into an augmented triad. You'll hear this sound crop up frequently as we begin to develop melodic lines with this arpeggio.

Example 5p

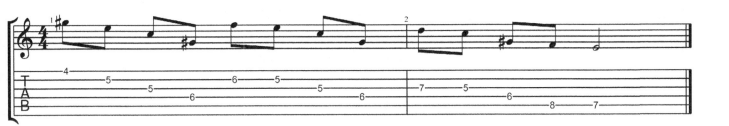

Here's a simple line that feels like a pentatonic lick and nicely spells the sound of the arpeggio.

Example 5q

Next, we move to some lines built from the #5 (C) of E7#5b9.

The first line is arranged around 1st position.

Example 5r

The next line works well as a rapid ascending lick. You'll need to execute position shifts on the fourth and second strings, both played with the second finger.

Example 5s

The final #5 line has a bigger position shift on the second string. You can either quickly jump your fretting hand forward, or execute the position shift with a slide as indicated in the TAB.

Example 5t

Now let's play some lines built from the b7 (D). This descending idea uses the E augmented sound at the beginning.

Example 5u

An augmented shape is hidden inside this line too.

Example 5v

Here's one more b7 line that begins in 10th position and works its way down to resolve on the fourth string root at the 2nd fret.

Example 5w

To finish this section, here are three lines built from the b9 (F).

In bar two of this line, we take advantage of the small chord shapes that exist within the arpeggio pattern. The first group of three notes spell Eaug, the next three imply E7#5 without its root, and the third are another inversion of Eaug.

Example 5x

Once you learn an arpeggio shape, it's easy to fall into playing similar patterns all the time, so this line avoids the obvious "next note" to take a more interesting path.

Example 5y

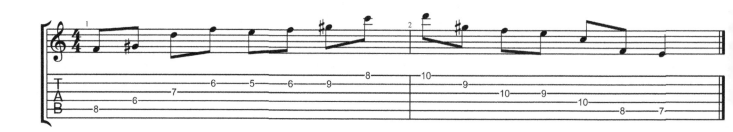

The final b9 line uses an interval skip in bar one to break it up and restart its linear descent.

Example 5z

Targeting arpeggio tones with passing notes

Now it's time to get more creative with this arpeggio and turn it into musical licks. As with the minor 7b5 chord, this arpeggio already has a strong identity – the #5 and b9 intervals take care of that. We don't, therefore, want to obscure its character by bombarding it with chromatic notes – that would be counterproductive. Instead we'll add occasional passing notes, just to spice things up.

This first lick places a passing note between the D and C arpeggio tones at the beginning, and from the middle of bar two uses chromatic approach notes a half step below the C and G#.

Example 5z1

This line begins with a fast chromatic run down, but thereafter it's all arpeggio tones. Play the first four notes with a one-finger-per-fret pattern, then slide the first finger down one fret to play the 4th.

Example 5z2

In this example, an approach note is used on beat 1 to target the E root. The same thing happens at the beginning of bar two. Rhythmic variety is introduced to make the end of this line more interesting and bar three adds one more passing note.

Example 5z3

The next example combines 1/8th note triplets with a fast descending 1/16th note line. The augmented triad appears again in bar one's triplet passage. You can move this augmented shape around the fretboard in major 3rds (four frets), hence we can start it from the 4th, 8th and 12th frets. In bar two there are more chromatic notes this time to keep the line flowing, but the last three notes spell Eaug again.

Example 5z4

In bar one of this lick we follow a pattern of half step movements. The first two are both arpeggio tones (E, F), but sticking to the pattern means that next, an arpeggio tone leads to a passing note, which is unusual. The chromatic run at the end of bar two targets the E root note in bar three.

Example 5z5

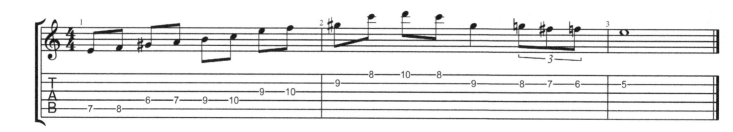

Next we have a more ambitious lick to dig into that begins with a 1/16th note run and transitions into 1/8th note triplets. There are just a couple of passing notes here that serve to keep up the momentum of the line.

Example 5z6

Next, a simple line with two passing notes. The target of this line is the b7 (D) at the end.

Example 5z7

Here's a line that has a repeating motif that gets modified in bar two and ends by highlighting the root note.

Example 5z8

This lick has a bluesy flavour at the beginning and becomes more linear in bars 3-4, targeting the 3rd (G#) at the end.

Example 5z9

Example 5z10 takes a more complex approach with passing notes that enclose the arpeggio tones. The end target of this line was the b7 (D), which although it's a chord tone still sounds slightly unresolved.

Example 5z10

For the next lick, let's go nuts with the augmented side of this arpeggio. In bar one, use all downward pick strokes and in bar two, all upward pick strokes until the end of the 1/8th note triplets.

Example 5z11

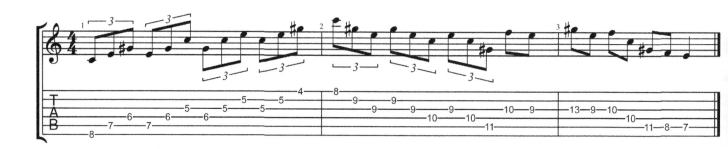

To end this chapter, here's a line that uses only one passing note and retains the strong flavour of the #5 and b9 character notes.

Example 5z12

Don't forget to refer to the appendix for the visual map of this arpeggio. It will remind you of the arpeggio's geography at a glance and is an invaluable tool when you want to compose licks.

Chapter Six – Major ii V I Arpeggio Vocabulary

In the final two chapters we're going to bring together all the arpeggio knowledge and practice of the previous chapters and turn it into usable licks you can play over the two most important chord progressions in jazz – the major and minor ii V I sequence. These cadences crop up in every single jazz standard (apart from modal tunes and straight three-chord blues), so it's essential to have some solid vocabulary for them under your fingers.

In this chapter I've composed a variety of licks with a range of difficulty that you can add to your playing immediately. Some are simple, succinct ideas that perfectly spell out the chord changes, while others contain bebop-style passing notes and weave around the harmony.

Once you've worked through this set of major ii V I examples, you can create your own by referring back to earlier chapters and combining arpeggio licks and runs, adapting them to your taste.

The major ii V I sequence used here is Dm7 – G7 – Cmaj7.

We'll be using Dm9 (Chapter Two), G7b9 (Chapter Three) and Cmaj7 (Chapter One) arpeggios to create our melodic lines.

I want to start by showing you a simple 1/8th note example and explain how I arrived at this line. First listen to/play through the example.

Example 6a

To construct this idea, I used the fifth string root shape for Dm9 shown in Example 2c; for the G7, the sixth string root shape of G7b9 from Example 3a; and the fifth string box position shape from Example 1b for Cmaj7.

With those shapes in mind, I moved from one arpeggio to the next by choosing notes that weren't far apart and fell within easy reach in the same zone of the neck.

Example 6a is a serviceable lick, but very straightforward in that it contains only arpeggio tones and has zero passing notes. For the second example, I want to show you how you can take a "safe" sounding line like this and spice it up. Example 6b uses the exact same structure as Example 6a but adds passing notes and more rhythmic variation.

When composing your own licks, your aim should be to have a clear visualisation of the arpeggio structure your lick will be based around. Then you can add passing notes and rhythmic variations to create a more interesting melodic line.

Example 6b

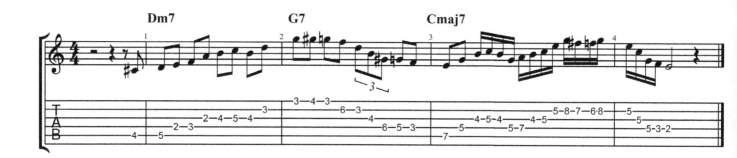

Now let's explore lots more major ii V I vocabulary.

This line descends the higher position Dm9 arpeggio, adding one C Major scale note (G) to complete the 1/8th note line. Then it ascends G7b9 and descends Cmaj7. A position change in bar three means that the line covers a wider range of the neck.

Example 6c

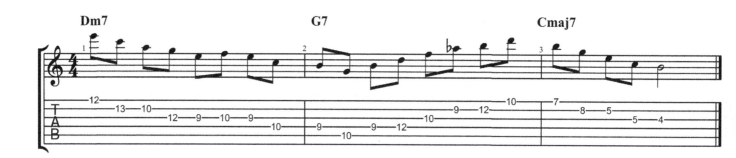

In previous chapters we practiced playing arpeggio lines from other chord tones apart from the root. In this example, the descending Dm9 line begins on the b3 (F), the G7b9 line begins on the 3rd (B) and the Cmaj7 line on the 5th (G).

Example 6d

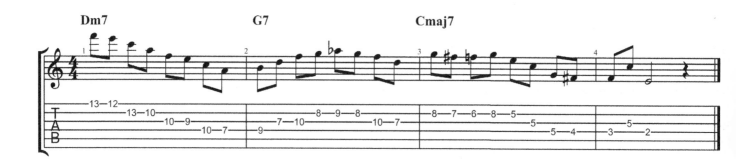

We can compose fresh lines using the principles we've learned, but we can also mine the examples of previous chapters and "assemble" licks by mixing and matching arpeggio lines. The next line combines bars from Example 2x, Example 3l and Example 1z5. I matched them by finding lines that began/ended on the same string.

Example 6e

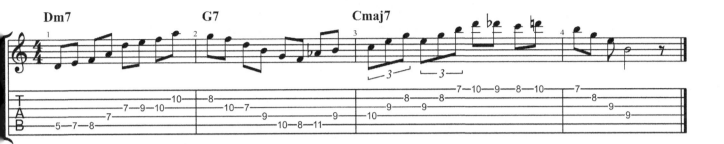

This line combines ideas from Example 2z1 for the Dm7 chord and Example 3z7 for the G7, then adds a completely new ending.

Example 6f

The next line contains just one passing note on the Dm7. It ascends the G7b9 arpeggio in traditional fashion, then the Cmaj7 arpeggio is sequenced into descending 1/16th note groups of four.

Example 6g

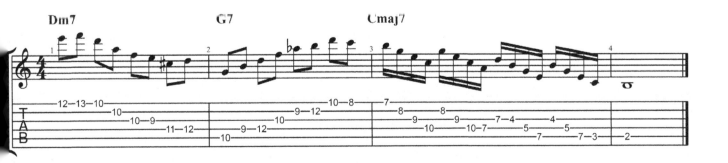

In jazz, soloists will sometimes disregard the ii chord in the ii V cadence and focus on an altered dominant sound for both bars. Here's a line that does that. Bars 1-2 use a section of Example 3z – a G7b9 sequence that moves in minor thirds.

When played over a Dm7 chord, this sounds more "outside". The G7b9 sequence contains two notes that don't belong to the Dm9 arpeggio we've worked with but they do imply other D minor chord variations. The B note, superimposed over Dm7 implies a Dm13 sound, and the Ab implies Dm7b5. Both create an interesting tension. The final surprise F note over Cmaj7 implies a Cmaj11 sound.

Example 6h

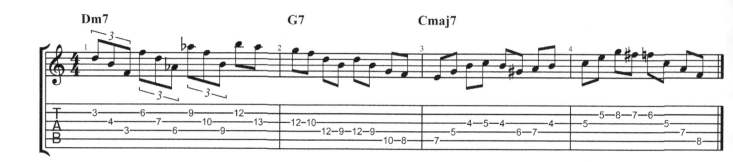

This next lick is a staple bebop line that dances around the changes.

Example 6i

Here's another, but this time we're breaking up the rhythm a little more.

Example 6j

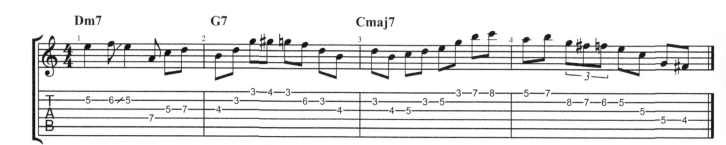

In this line, a chromatic run down targets the b3 of Dm7 in bar one. At the end of that bar, a half step movement connects the Dm9 arpeggio to G7b9. Whenever possible, a half step movement is a very strong way of resolving one arpeggio to the next. In this instance the 9th (B) of D minor resolves up a half step to the b7 (F) of G7. A similar resolution occurs in bars 2-3, where the b9 (Ab) of G7 resolves down a half step to the 5th (G) of Cmaj7.

Example 6k

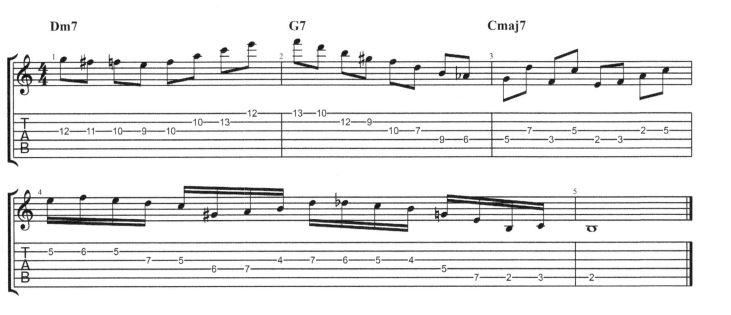

The next example uses a rhythmic motif to drive the melodic line. The phrase is the same each time as it moves through each arpeggio. To create the motif, I used shapes for each arpeggio that avoid the root note at the beginning.

Example 6l

In the next line, the use of the C# passing note in bar one suggests the sound of a Dmin(Maj7) chord.

Example 6m

In this more intervallic lick, fragments of the G7b9 arpeggio are picked out to give the line a more modern sound. Rhythmic variation throughout keeps things interesting.

Example 6n

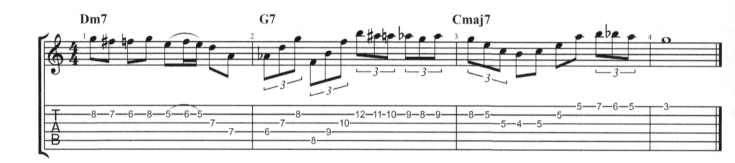

Here's another reminder that you can experiment by playing G7b9 arpeggio lines over both the ii and V chord. This lick has been transplanted from Example 3z9 in its entirety. Because it contains a couple of passing notes, when superimposed over the Dm7 chord it creates a lot of tension. The line ends on the root of the G7b9 arpeggio, which is also the 5th of Cmaj7.

Example 6o

This lick begins by emphasising the 5th (A) of Dm7, with chromatic notes enclosing. 1/8th note triplets and some space break up the phrase.

Example 6p

The next example is a simple line that succinctly spells out the changes, ending on the 3rd of Cmaj7.

Example 6q

This line uses the C# passing note over Dm7, each time to resolve to the root.

Example 6r

The Dm9 arpeggio shape that begins this lick is one that just falls naturally under the fingers and always sounds good. It's followed up by a Pat Martino style 1/16th note run.

Example 6s

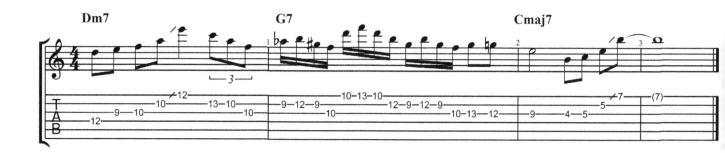

To end this chapter, here's an intervallic idea that descends through the changes as it travels down the fretboard.

Example 6t

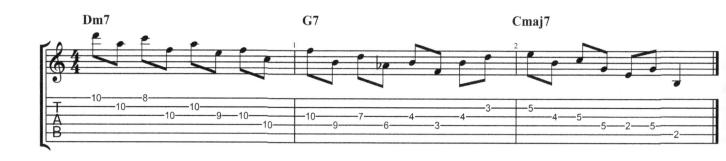

Chapter Seven – Minor ii V i Arpeggio Vocabulary

In this final chapter we have a collection of arpeggio lines played over a minor ii V i progression in the key of A Minor. On a jazz standard chord chart, you'll generally see this written as,

Bm7b5 – E7 – Am7

But remember we'll be soloing over it using Bm7b5, E7#5b9 and Am9 arpeggios.

Taking the same approach as the previous chapter, there are licks of varying difficulty. Some are improvised on the spot, while others take arpeggio lines from earlier chapters and combine them to create a lick. There is also a mix of lines that use predominantly arpeggio tones and lines that have more passing notes.

Once you've worked through this set of minor ii V i examples, look back over the lines from earlier chapters and work on creating your own combinations.

The first lick begins with a fairly straight Bm7b5 line using the sixth string root shape with one added passing note.

Example 7a

This line ascends from the fifth string root shape of Bm7b5, again with one added passing note. Bar two highlights a very clean way of outlining the E7#5b9 sound and can be played using pull-offs if you prefer. In bar three, the line is heading towards the target note of the 9th (B) of A minor.

Example 7b

This line utilises a couple of previous examples. Bar one has the Bm7b5 line from Example 4n and bar two the E7#5b9 line from Example 5n, fused together with a new ending.

Example 7c

In bar two of Example 7d we take advantage of the augmented character of the E7#5b9 chord, playing two inversions of E augmented. Bar one uses a similar idea over the Bm7b5 chord to set up what will happen in bar two, matching the phrasing. The idea continues for the first half of bar three before it resolves.

Example 7d

Next, here is a typical bebop line that contains more passing notes.

Example 7e

In bar one of this example, the Bm7b5 arpeggio is played in triplet clusters, then moves into a straight 1/16th note run. I actually used a complete Bm7b5 line for bars one and two here, rather than playing the E7#5b9 arpeggio over the E7 chord. So, what is the result of superimposing Bm7b5 over E7? There are only four individual notes that make up bar two: B, A, F and C. Over E7 the are the 5th, 11th, b9 and b13 intervals respectively, giving the E7 an extended/altered sound. It's the reverse idea of playing an altered dominant sound over both ii and V chords.

Example 7f

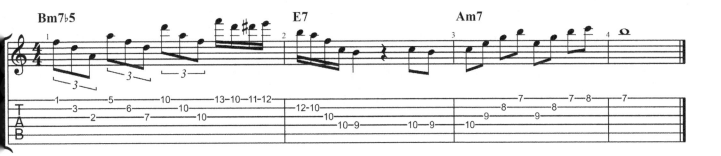

To play bar two of this next line, I recommend the following fingering: play the first string 8th fret with the first finger, and the second string 9th fret with the second finger, then hop the first finger over to play the third string, 9th fret. Leave the first finger barring the second and third strings at the 9th for the next part of the phrase.

You could hold down the augmented chord shape for the first four notes of bar two, but I find the above fingering gives much better note separation in the sound.

Similarly, in bar three, barre the third and fourth strings at the 9th with the first finger to play the first six notes, then hop the first finger over to the second string 8th fret, and again onto the first string 7th fret.

Example 7g

This bebop-orientated line uses just two chromatic approach notes from a half step below for the Bm7b5 chord.

Example 7h

Example 7i is another line where bars 1-2 are all Bm7b5 arpeggio notes. Over E7 they imply an extended/altered chord. For the Am7 bar we have a line built in 4th intervals. The D note in the second half of the bar is the only non-arpeggio note, included to continue the pattern of 4ths.

Example 7i

Now for a quite different style of lick that strays in jazz fusion territory (though you can still use it in a straight-ahead jazz setting for dramatic effect).

The idea here is to capture the sound of each chord with as few arpeggio notes as possible. In bar one we have the b3, b5 and root of the Bm7b5. Bar two uses the b9, 3rd and b7 of E7 (the #5 note doesn't feature in this lick). The Am7 lick is built around the 9th, b7 and root. The added D note is the 11th.

The easiest way to play this lick is using hammer-ons and pull-offs as indicated. In bar one, strike the second string with a pick downstroke to start the lick, then pick downwards from the third to second string, repeatedly pushing through the strings. Bar two has an identical picking action, as does bar three but on the second/first strings.

It's good to practice this one slowly to begin with, to get clear note separation.

Example 7j

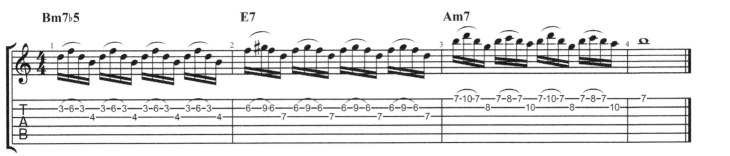

By way of contrast, here's a laidback cool-jazz lick that defines the harmony with a few notes and makes use of space.

Example 7k

This lick exploits the augmented pattern within E7#5b9.

Example 7l

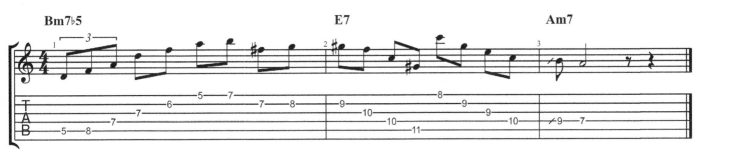

This example begins with a line that uses chromatic approach notes to connect the b3 and root of Bm7b5. In bar two, a descending E7#5b9 run resolves a half step to the 5th of Am7 in bar three.

Example 7m

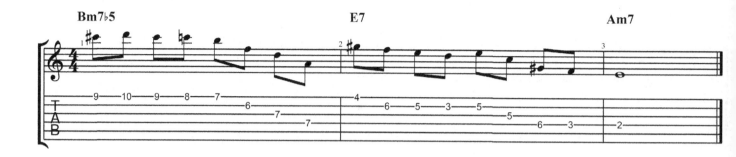

This lick features a fast descending E7#5b9 run in bar two. At the end of bar one, a single chromatic approach note sets it up. At the end of the run, a half step movement connects to the Am9 arpeggio.

Example 7n

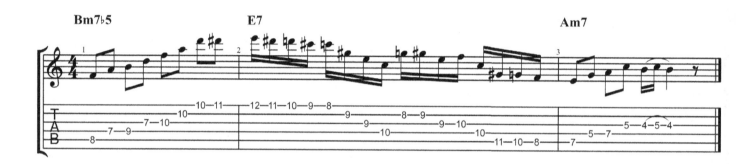

Here's a more challenging lick that begins with the fast 1/16th note Bm7b5 run first seen in Example 4z6, fuses it together with the E7#5b9 1/16th note run from Example 5z4, and adds a new ending.

Hammer-ons on used at strategic points throughout the lick aid fretting hand position shifts and give it a more legato feel. In the second half of bar three, to contend with the 1/16th note triplets, I used hammer-ons for the first group, a downward pick rake for the second group, then a second string hammer-on in the last group before sliding into the high E.

Break it down bar by bar and work out the most economical fingering before bringing it up to tempo.

Example 7o

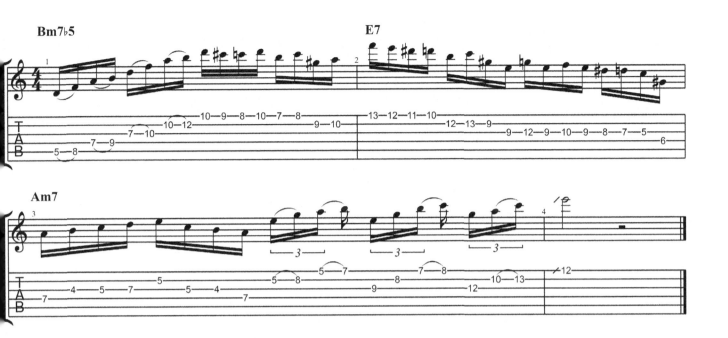

Next up is a descending triplet idea.

Example 7p

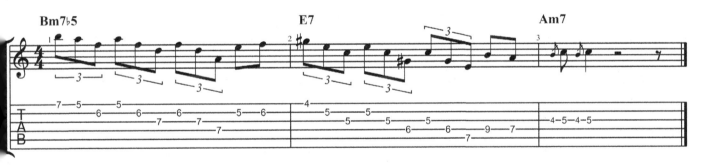

This example again uses the tactic of treating the ii and V chords as the same tonality. The line in bars 1-2 is all E7#5b9 arpeggio notes. The effect of this is to imply extended or altered tones over the Bm7b5 chord, such as the 11th, 13th and b9. It creates some nice tension to precede the E7 chord.

Example 7q

Example 7r uses the same idea. The E7alt arpeggio begins on a D note, which happens to be the b3 of Bm7b5. The G# note, used twice in bar one, implies a richer Bm13b5 harmony.

Example 7r

For the final example it's back to spelling out each chord with its own arpeggio. After the initial burst of 1/16th notes we move into straight 1/8th notes with a routine ascent of E7#5b9 and a sequenced Am9 arpeggio pattern.

Example 7s

Appendix – Fretboard Maps

In this appendix, I've included fretboard maps for the major and minor ii V I chords we've been working with. Many of the world's best jazz guitarists have said that when they think of a chord (e.g. Cmaj7), while they are playing on that chord the whole fretboard becomes "Cmaj7" at that moment. If you can work towards achieving that kind of visualisation in your playing, then you'll have great freedom to play whatever you want, anywhere on the neck.

I suggest using these fretboard maps in two ways:

1. Focus on one just chord and study its geography on the neck. Within the shape you'll see patterns that reoccur, around which you can build melodic ideas. Players like Kurt Rosenwinkel and Julian Lage use these patterns to navigate the range of the neck and play more interesting ideas, using fragments that make the "sound" of the chord.

2. Use these maps to build your own ii V I lines. When you come up with, let's say, a nice Dm9 line, you can then refer to the G7b9 map to see how you can connect to that arpeggio in a seamless, musical way. You might rely on the maps for a while, but soon you'll begin to hear and visualise the intervals on the guitar neck without them.

There are plenty of online tools you can use to create your own maps of other chords for practice. Take your favourite jazz standard, map out the chords, then really go to town on it.

Dm9

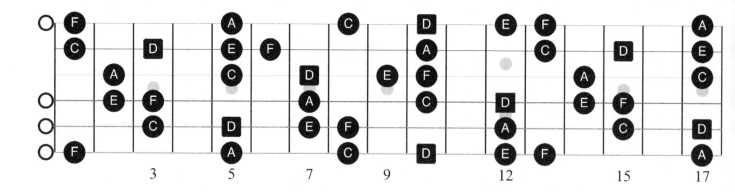

G7b9

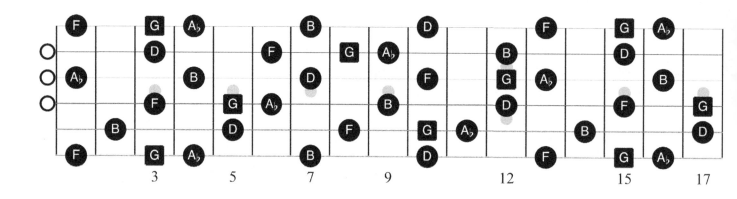

Cmaj7

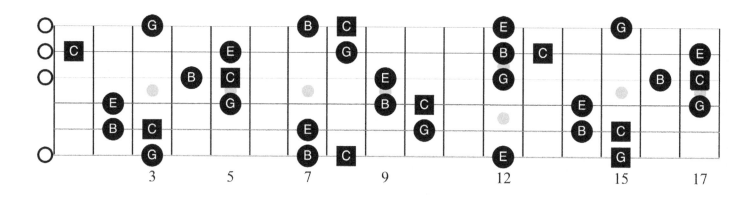

Bm7b5

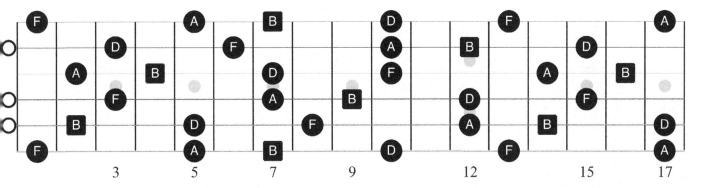

E7#5b9

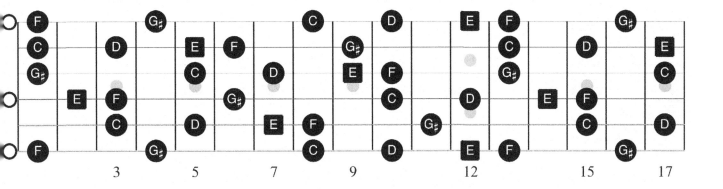

Am9

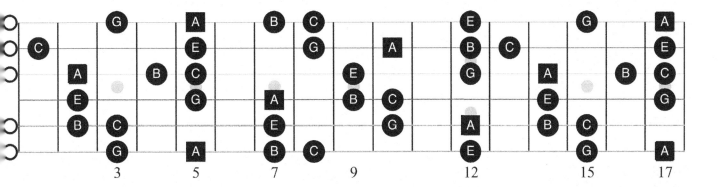

By the Same Author

Jazz Bebop Blues Guitar

• Major / Minor scale and arpeggio substitutions to create melodic jazz lines

• A creative jazz-blues guitar method that will help you play great licks straight away

• Lines in the style of Joe Pass, Wes Montgomery, Jim Hall and Pat Martino

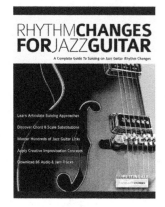

Rhythm Changes for Jazz Guitar

A Creative Guide to Soloing On Rhythm Changes for Jazz Guitar

• Get inside one of the most important jazz guitar chord sequences

• An in-depth guide to improvising over Rhythm Changes with tons of substitution ideas

• Learn hundreds of well-conceived melodic jazz guitar licks

Jazz Guitar Chord Creativity

• A systematic approach to playing any jazz chord in any position on the neck

• Unlock fluid, creative freedom when you comp and use the full range of the guitar neck

• Connect cascading chord sequences across every "zone" of the guitar neck to master true jazz guitar voice leading

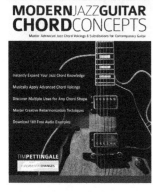

Modern Jazz Guitar Chord Concepts

Modern Jazz Guitar Chord Concepts walks you through the most useful altered and extended major, minor and dominant chord structures, while teaching you multiple voicings for each that can be used in real musical situations. This comprehensive guide provides a creative method that gets you playing real music from page one, anywhere on the neck.

Made in the USA
Las Vegas, NV
11 May 2023

71903671R00057